romans

the epistle of paul the apostle to the

romans

authorised king james version

printed by authority

published by canongate

with an introduction by | ruth rendell

First published in Great Britain in 1999
by Canongate Books Ltd
14 High Street, Edinburgh EH1 1TE

10 9 8 7 6 5 4 3 2 1

Introduction copyright © Ruth Rendell 1999
The moral right of the author has been asserted

British Library Cataloguing-in-Publication Data
A catalogue record is available on request from
the British Library

ISBN 0 86241 972 7

Typeset by Palimpsest Book Production
Book design by Paddy Cramsie at et al
Printed and bound in Great Britain
by Caledonian International, Bishopbriggs

a note about pocket canons

The Authorised King James Version of the Bible, translated between 1603–11, coincided with an extraordinary flowering of English literature. This version, more than any other, and possibly more than any other work in history, has had an influence in shaping the language we speak and write today.

Twenty-four of the eighty original books of the King James Bible are brought to you in this series. They encompass categories as diverse as history, philosophy, law, poetry and fiction. Each Pocket Canon also has its own introduction, specially commissioned from an impressive range of writers, to provide a personal interpretation of the text and explore its contemporary relevance.

introduction by ruth rendell

Ruth Rendell is the author of more than forty novels, among them the Inspector Wexford series, and six volumes of short stories. She also writes under the pseudonym Barbara Vine. Many of her books have been adapted for television and feature films based on her work have been made by Claude Chabrol and Pedro Almodovar. She has received numerous fiction prizes, including the Arts Council's National Book Award for Genre Fiction, four Gold Daggers from the Crime Writers' Association, the Edgar Allan Poe Award and the Angel Award for Fiction. Ruth Rendell received a CBE in 1996 and in the following year was made a Life Peer. Her latest novel is A Sight for Sore Eyes.

The Road to Damascus is a phrase which has entered our language and our literature, becoming a metaphor for the sort of life-changing experience which strikes with suddenness and leaves its object transformed. It first happened to Paul the Apostle whose course of life, beliefs and objectives were all overturned by what happened to him on that actual road to that actual city.

He is believed to have been born in Tarsus, now part of Turkey, and was a Roman Citizen, a useful status which conferred certain judicial privileges, including that of *appellatio*, appeal to Caesar himself. He spoke Greek as his mother tongue, but in his letters he refers to his Jewishness – he had been a rabbinical student. Yet by profession he was a tentmaker, a trade somewhat frowned upon by strict Judaic orthodoxy. It will be seen that there were inconsistencies in his early life which modern scholars cannot account for and mysteries they cannot solve.

What is beyond doubt is that he was initially at the fore-front of those who persecuted the Christians of Jerusalem. He might have been a temple guard and may possibly have been present at the arrest and crucifixion of Jesus. Certain it is that he played a significant part in the stoning of Stephen, a devout and active Christian. Stephen died and Paul 'made havoc of the [Christian] church, and entering every house and haling men and women, committed them to prison' (*Acts* 8:3). He asked the high priest for letters to the synagogues of Damascus, there to root out trouble-makers and bring them back as prisoners to Jerusalem. It was on this journey that the event took place which so immediately and entirely converted him.

Here, at one moment, we have a rabid oppressor and man of violence, 'breathing out threatenings and slaughter against the disciples of the Lord' (*Acts* 9:1), at the next the most obedient and devout of those disciples and an undoubted founder of the Christian religion. It is rather as if a camp guard suddenly became merciful to the inmates of Auschwitz and survived to become a great philosopher.

What happened to Paul on his Road to Damascus? Was he an epileptic, as some say, and this his first seizure? Had he been overworking and become, as we might put it today, 'stressed-out'? Or did he really hear the bidding of God? *Acts* says and he says himself that he saw a bright light and fell down, heard a voice call him by name and ask him, 'Why persecutest thou me?' (*Acts* 9:4) Paul inquired who this was and the voice replied he was Jesus and said, 'It is hard for thee to kick against the pricks.' The metaphor, of course, is that of the ass or ox kicking against the stings of the goad and the meaning that the speaker understood Saul's difficulties and the promptings of his conscience. From that moment, Saul now called Paul, saw himself as appointed to bear Christ's name 'before the Gentiles, and kings, and the children of Israel' (*Acts* 8:3).

He was somewhere between twenty and thirty years old, a small hook-nosed, bandy-legged man, humble and proud, brave and meek, the prisoner, as he joyfully (and sometimes with anguish) called himself, of Jesus Christ. Although he would have preferred everyone to be as he was, celibate and unencumbered by a family, he advocated marriage as 'honourable to all'. After his conversion he became a missionary and he wrote his epistles, thus becoming one of the greatest letter-writers the world has ever known and propounding principles and precepts of a startling originality. Of these the letter he wrote to the Romans, meaning to the Christians or 'church' of Rome, is generally thought the finest and perhaps the only one of whose sole and consistent authorship we can be certain.

Paul wrote this letter while staying in Corinth, capital of the Greek province of Achaia, during the cold months of the year, very probably a winter in the late fifties AD. When it was finished he appointed a woman called Phebe to carry it to Rome. In the final chapter, he asks its recipients to receive Phebe in a way becoming to them and to give her whatever assistance she may ask for, thus somewhat weakening the arguments of those critics who down the ages have called him a misogynist and despiser of women. Phebe must have travelled to Rome by sea, bringing to the beleaguered servants of the Roman church a foundation document of the faith.

Only by reading *Romans* in the knowledge of the kind of world Paul lived in can his letter be more fully understood. The Roman dominance of the known world was one of the most oppressive tyrannies nations have ever lived under. A huge proportion of the population was enslaved and few Romans, if any, thought of slavery as wrong. Punishment for any offences in the area of sedition was draconian. The Emperor Claudius had expelled the Jews from Rome and in a few years' time Titus was to sack Jerusalem, destroy the Temple and scatter the people of Israel. It was a superstitious world where sorcerers abounded, where signs and portents were part of everyday life, where cults of all kinds flourished, and where great religious ceremonies centred on blood sacrifice.

Today to believers, agnostics and atheists alike, crucifixion is a word both awesome and commonplace and one that brings to mind a single event: the execution of Jesus Christ. The sign of the cross is indicative of Christianity, and the idea of the cross is ineluctably bound up with Christ's death. But if we think about that death at all, even the most indifferent to the faith it gave rise to, think of it as honourable, a unique martyrdom. Anyone who travelled the Roman Empire at that time would have seen crosses on which the dead or dying hung, comparable perhaps to roadside gallows bearing their decaying corpses in mediaeval Britain. And to everyone, including Paul himself, crucifixion was a disgraceful manner of death, so that it is all the more extraordinary that he could write as he does in his letter to the Galatians, 'God forbid that I should glory save in the cross of our Lord Jesus Christ' (*Galatians* 6:14).

But perhaps the most important fact readers of this letter should know before they begin it, is how early it appears in the scheme of writings which form the New Testament. Most assume, and understandably, that the Gospels come first, then the *Acts of the Apostles* and after that the *Epistles of Paul*. Thus, Paul would have been writing with the Gospels as his source material. But none of those books existed when he set down his knowledge and beliefs. The earliest of the Gospels, that of *Mark*, cannot have been composed much before 70 AD, and by that time Paul's literary output was over and he was most probably dead. If readers today find a number of his precepts familiar, this is because they have come across them before, in church, in Sunday school, in literature and enshrined in Christian philosophy, as owing their provenance to the Gospels. But Paul came first.

Authorities have been commenting on *Romans* for nearly two thousand years. Every word Paul wrote in his letter has been minutely examined, both in translation and in the original, with commentators probing Greek prepositions and classical usage, in an effort to shed light on unfathomable obscurities. We shall approach it more humbly, remembering always that when Paul wrote it Jesus Christ had been crucified only about twenty-five years before.

He begins in the classical Greek fashion of starting a letter, with his name and his vocation: 'Paul, a servant of Jesus Christ, called to be an apostle,' then sets down the tenets of his faith. Kind and comforting messages for his letter's recipients follow; he mentions them always in his prayers and says how he longs to see them. Paul has never been to Rome but he intends to go, hoping for a safe journey in order to preach in person while there. He tells them he is not ashamed of the Gospel (in its sense of the good news). A tradition of shame prevails towards Christianity because Christ came not in majesty but in a way likely to be looked on as abjection and foolishness. Paul knows that this apparently weak message is in fact the supreme power of God himself directed towards man's salvation.

Faith can arise only through human beings' close contact with the Gospel. Paul explains the disastrous progress of evil in society as the natural process of cause and effect, not as the direct act of God. His first chapter ends with an exposure of certain kinds of 'unrighteousness' and here we come upon our first major difficulty in interpreting exactly what he meant. Through the ages men have taken six verses in particular to mean that all homosexuality was abhorrent to Christianity, 'men with men working that which is unseemly' being a phrase on which it is hard to put any other construction. Paul would have known of the importance of homosexuality in Greek thought where homosexual love was often glorified as superior to the heterosexual; he also knew that it was an abomination to the Jews which may be the reason for his harsh denunciations. Throughout his letters, though he comes to regard circumcision as unnecessary and certain dietary laws superfluous, and of course is confident that the Messiah has come, he otherwise holds fast to the Jewish Law. Certain authorities have sought to emphasise that his invective may be directed only against physical abuse in the kind of cult ceremonies Paul, coming as he did from Tarsus, would have been well acquainted with. Readers must draw their own conclusions.

The last four lines of the first chapter are interesting in a quite different way. They can be interpreted as meaning that those who watch, applaud and approve wrongdoing in others, though doing none themselves, are more guilty than those who commit it. An example would be that of the dictator who, rather than carry out torture himself, allow its use by his security forces and looks on with approbation.

He follows directly with a denunciation of hypocrisy. God will render to every man according to how he has behaved, for He cares nothing for rank, riches or status, and is no respecter of persons. Perhaps it is at this point that we should remind ourselves that Paul was not writing for believers living centuries after Christ. He had no doubt that the end of the world was at hand, as had all Christians of his day, and to him the Second Coming was a reality to be expected at any moment. Therefore repentance, amendment of behaviour and a full knowledge of God and Jesus are matters of urgency. Circumcision, he tells us, is of no use in itself, the physical act that is, but 'circumcision is that of the heart'. In other words, to have faith is most important of all, but being a Jew (i.e. a circumcised person) matters too, the rite of circumcision affecting the spirit as well as the flesh, because it was to the Jews originally that the oracles of God were sent by Moses. All men, however, Jew and Gentile alike, are sinners and Jews need not think themselves better than the rest of the world.

Inheritance of the world was promised to Abraham and his descendants, and this gift was made not on condition that it was merited through fulfilment of the law, but simply on the basis of the rightness of the faith they upheld. The relevance to all Christians is in Abraham's faith as the paradigm of their own. It was quite a new thought that Abraham was the father of all who believe, not only of the Jews. But if those who have a claim to the inheritance do so on the basis of their obedience to the law alone, they will be disappointed, since no one is truly obedient but Christ Himself. Against all hope Abraham continued to believe in God's promise that he would be the ancestor of many nations, even though he and his wife were old and childless. By the conception and birth of his son Isaac his faith was proved. Just as he never doubted God's promise, so we must never doubt it.

Man's parent-and-child relationship with God is integral to forgiveness and absolution, and his purpose for humanity is altogether merciful. We were enemies of God, but by the death of his son became his friends, thus atonement through Christ should be a source of joy. (In the next chapter Paul points out that while it is rare for someone to give his life to save even a good man, and not much rarer to do so for someone who has been his benefactor, Christ died for the wicked.) But at the very place where sin most outrageously abounded, in Israel's rejection of Jesus, there grace abounded more and triumphed gloriously. Certain people would draw the inference that we must go on sinning that grace may be multiplied, but this Paul rejects utterly.

At the moment someone receives baptism, the dying and rising again of Christ takes place in him without any co-operation or exercise of will on his part. Baptism is a pledge of that death which, in God's sight, the person concerned has already succumbed to and of resurrection through union with Christ. Martin Luther, in his commentary, said that it was as if Paul 'wanted to give us impressive proof of the fact that … every word in the Bible points to Christ.' Israel, says Paul, has misunderstood the law because it failed to comprehend that this was what it was all about.

Paul instructs the Romans on how to behave, and the Commandments not to kill, commit adultery, steal, bear false witness or covet are all summed up in the instruction to love one's neighbour as oneself. But one's enemy also must be loved. If an enemy is hungry, feed him, if thirsty, give him drink, for to do so is to heap 'coals of fire' on his head. The expression probably derives from the Egyptian ritual in which a man purged his offence by carrying on his head a dish containing burning charcoal on a bed of ashes. Paul goes on to speak of the imminence of the second coming, for the ministry of Jesus had ushered in the last days, the End-time. History's supreme events had taken place through Christ's life, death and resurrection.

Returning to one of his central themes, Paul has more to say about Judaism and Christianity. Dietary rules are no longer important. Now Christ's work on earth is done, the situation with regard to the ceremonial part of Old Testament eating and abstaining has been radically transformed. One obeys it by believing in him to whom it bears witness. Keep from hurting others with your dietary rules and remember that the Kingdom of God is not a matter of eating and drinking. But the strong Christian will not boast of his superior knowledge in this area. Paul explains that not everything which is delightful is to be avoided but one should not please oneself regardless of its effect on others.

He ends with greetings to a great many people and here women (Priscilla, Mary, Junia, Tryphena, Tryphosa, Julia, the sister of Nereus and the mother of Rufus) are accorded at least the same affection and admiration as men. Paul seems here to have tried to attach expressions of kindly commendation to all the individuals he mentions. At the end of this last chapter Tertius's declaration that he 'wrote this epistle' means not that he was its author but most probably that he wrote it from Paul's dictation.

What became of Paul? No one knows. The likelihood is that his fate was unknown even then, or Luke, who wrote the *Acts*, might have told us. What is known is that Paul came up for trial in Jerusalem and appealed, as he had the right to do, to Caesar. He was taken to the city to which he directed his letter and seems to have appeared twice before that Emperor whose very name causes a chill, Nero. In Rome he lived for two years under house arrest and the second of the letters to Timothy which bears his name sometimes includes the rather sinister note: '... written from Rome, when Paul was brought before Nero the second time.' Perhaps he died a martyr's death. No one can be sure. But if he did he would not have been thrown to wild beasts or made a human torch, but beheaded with a sword, as was prescribed for a Roman Citizen. He left behind him a book which is a blueprint for Christianity. Believers and non-believers alike cannot help but be stricken with awe by its temerity and Paul's genius.

the epistle of paul the apostle to the romans

Paul, a servant of Jesus Christ, called to be an apostle, separated unto the gospel of God ²(which he had promised afore by his prophets in the holy scriptures), ³concerning his Son Jesus Christ our Lord, which was made of the seed of David according to the flesh, ⁴and declared to be the Son of God with power, according to the spirit of holiness, by the resurrection from the dead, ⁵by whom we have received grace and apostleship, for obedience to the faith among all nations, for his name, ⁶among whom are ye also the called of Jesus Christ:

⁷To all that be in Rome, beloved of God, called to be saints: Grace to you and peace from God our Father, and the Lord Jesus Christ.

⁸First, I thank my God through Jesus Christ for you all, that your faith is spoken of throughout the whole world. ⁹For God is my witness, whom I serve with my spirit in the gospel of his Son, that without ceasing I make mention of you always in my prayers; ¹⁰making request, if by any means now at length I might have a prosperous journey by the will of God to come unto you. ¹¹For I long to see you, that I may impart unto you some spiritual gift, to the end ye may be established; ¹²That is, that I may be comforted together with you by the mutual faith both of you and me. ¹³Now I would not have you ignorant, brethren, that oftentimes I purposed to come unto you (but was let hitherto), that I might have some fruit among you also, even

as among other Gentiles. [14] I am debtor both to the Greeks, and to the Barbarians; both to the wise, and to the unwise. [15] So, as much as in me is, I am ready to preach the gospel to you that are at Rome also.

[16] For I am not ashamed of the gospel of Christ, for it is the power of God unto salvation to every one that believeth; to the Jew first, and also to the Greek. [17] For therein is the righteousness of God revealed from faith to faith, as it is written, 'The just shall live by faith'.

[18] For the wrath of God is revealed from heaven against all ungodliness and unrighteousness of men, who hold the truth in unrighteousness, [19] because that which may be known of God is manifest in them, for God hath shewed it unto them. [20] For the invisible things of him from the creation of the world are clearly seen, being understood by the things that are made, even his eternal power and Godhead; so that they are without excuse, [21] because that, when they knew God, they glorified him not as God, neither were thankful; but became vain in their imaginations, and their foolish heart was darkened. [22] Professing themselves to be wise, they became fools, [23] and changed the glory of the uncorruptible God into an image made like to corruptible man, and to birds, and four-footed beasts, and creeping things. [24] Wherefore God also gave them up to uncleanness through the lusts of their own hearts, to dishonour their own bodies between themselves, [25] who changed the truth of God into a lie, and worshipped and served the creature more than the Creator, who is blessed for ever. Amen.

[26] For this cause God gave them up unto vile affections, for even their women did change the natural use into that which is against nature: [27] And likewise also the men, leaving the natural

use of the woman, burned in their lust one toward another; men with men working that which is unseemly, and receiving in themselves that recompence of their error which was meet. ²⁸And even as they did not like to retain God in their knowledge, God gave them over to a reprobate mind, to do those things which are not convenient; ²⁹being filled with all unrighteousness, fornication, wickedness, covetousness, maliciousness; full of envy, murder, debate, deceit, malignity; whisperers, ³⁰backbiters, haters of God, despiteful, proud, boasters, inventors of evil things, disobedient to parents, ³¹without understanding, covenant-breakers, without natural affection, implacable, unmerciful, ³²who knowing the judgment of God, that they which commit such things are worthy of death, not only do the same, but have pleasure in them that do them.

2 Therefore thou art inexcusable, O man, whosoever thou art that judgest; for wherein thou judgest another, thou condemnest thyself; for thou that judgest doest the same things. ²But we are sure that the judgment of God is according to truth against them which commit such things. ³And thinkest thou this, O man, that judgest them which do such things, and does the same, that thou shalt escape the judgment of God? ⁴Or despisest thou the riches of his goodness and forbearance and longsuffering; not knowing that the goodness of God leadeth thee to repentance? ⁵But after thy hardness and impenitent heart treasurest up unto thyself wrath against the day of wrath and revelation of the righteous judgment of God; ⁶who will render to every man according to his deeds: ⁷to them who by patient continuance in well doing seek for glory and honour and immortality, eternal life: ⁸but unto them that are con-

tentious, and do not obey the truth, but obey unrighteousness, indignation and wrath, ⁹ tribulation and anguish, upon every soul of man that doeth evil, of the Jew first, and also of the Gentile; ¹⁰ but glory, honour, and peace, to every man that worketh good, to the Jew first, and also to the Gentile, ¹¹ for there is no respect of persons with God.

¹² For as many as have sinned without law shall also perish without law: and as many as have sinned in the law shall be judged by the law ¹³ (for not the hearers of the law are just before God, but the doers of the law shall be justified. ¹⁴ For when the Gentiles, which have not the law, do by nature the things contained in the law, these, having not the law, are a law unto themselves, ¹⁵ which shew the work of the law written in their hearts, their conscience also bearing witness, and their thoughts the mean while accusing or else excusing one another), ¹⁶ in the day when God shall judge the secrets of men by Jesus Christ according to my gospel.

¹⁷ Behold, thou art called a Jew, and restest in the law, and makest thy boast of God, ¹⁸ and knowest his will, and approvest the things that are more excellent, being instructed out of the law; ¹⁹ and art confident that thou thyself art a guide of the blind, a light of them which are in darkness, ²⁰ an instructor of the foolish, a teacher of babes, which hast the form of knowledge and of the truth in the law. ²¹ Thou therefore which teachest another, teachest thou not thyself? Thou that preachest a man should not steal, dost thou steal? ²² Thou that sayest a man should not commit adultery, dost thou commit adultery? Thou that abhorrest idols, dost thou commit sacrilege? ²³ Thou that makest thy boast of the law, through breaking the law dishonourest thou God? ²⁴ For the name of God is blasphemed among the Gentiles

through you, as it is written.

²⁵ For circumcision verily profiteth, if thou keep the law, but if thou be a breaker of the law, thy circumcision is made uncircumcision. ²⁶ Therefore if the uncircumcision keep the righteousness of the law, shall not his uncircumcision be counted for circumcision? ²⁷ And shall not uncircumcision which is by nature, if it fulfil the law, judge thee, who by the letter and circumcision dost transgress the law? ²⁸ For he is not a Jew, which is one outwardly; neither is that circumcision, which is outward in the flesh; ²⁹ but he is a Jew, which is one inwardly; and circumcision is that of the heart, in the spirit, and not in the letter; whose praise is not of men, but of God.

3 What advantage then hath the Jew? Or what profit is there of circumcision? ² Much every way: chiefly, because that unto them were committed the oracles of God. ³ For what if some did not believe? Shall their unbelief make the faith of God without effect? ⁴ God forbid: yea, let God be true, but every man a liar; as it is written, that thou mightest be justified in thy sayings, and mightest overcome when thou art judged. ⁵ But if our unrighteousness commend the righteousness of God, what shall we say? Is God unrighteous who taketh vengeance? (I speak as a man.) ⁶ God forbid, for then how shall God judge the world? ⁷ For if the truth of God hath more abounded through my lie unto his glory; why yet am I also judged as a sinner? ⁸ And not rather (as we be slanderously reported, and as some affirm that we say), 'Let us do evil, that good may come'? whose damnation is just.

⁹ What then? Are we better than they? No, in no wise, for we have before proved both Jews and Gentiles, that they are all

under sin, [10] as it is written, 'There is none righteous, no, not one; [11] there is none that understandeth, there is none that seeketh after God. [12] They are all gone out of the way, they are together become unprofitable; there is none that doeth good, no, not one.' [13] 'Their throat is an open sepulchre; with their tongues they have used deceit the poison of asps is under their lips.' [14] 'Whose mouth is full of cursing and bitterness.' [15] 'Their feet are swift to shed blood: [16] destruction and misery are in their ways: [17] and the way of peace have they not known.' [18] 'There is no fear of God before their eyes.'

[19] Now we know that what things soever the law saith, it saith to them who are under the law, that every mouth may be stopped, and all the world may become guilty before God. [20] Therefore by the deeds of the law there shall no flesh be justified in his sight, for by the law is the knowledge of sin.

[21] But now the righteousness of God without the law is manifested, being witnessed by the law and the prophets; [22] even the righteousness of God which is by faith of Jesus Christ unto all and upon all them that believe, for there is no difference, [23] for all have sinned, and come short of the glory of God; [24] being justified freely by his grace through the redemption that is in Christ Jesus, [25] whom God hath set forth to be a propitiation through faith in his blood, to declare his righteousness for the remission of sins that are past, through the forbearance of God; [26] to declare, I say, at this time his righteousness, that he might be just, and the justifier of him which believeth in Jesus.

[27] Where is boasting then? It is excluded. By what law? Of works? Nay, but by the law of faith. [28] Therefore we conclude that a man is justified by faith without the deeds of the law. [29] Is he the God of the Jews only? Is he not also of the Gentiles? Yes,

of the Gentiles also, [30] seeing it is one God, which shall justify the circumcision by faith, and uncircumcision through faith. [31] Do we then make void the law through faith? God forbid: yea, we establish the law.

4 What shall we say then that Abraham our father, as pertaining to the flesh, hath found? [2] For if Abraham were justified by works, he hath whereof to glory; but not before God. [3] For what saith the scripture? 'Abraham believed God, and it was counted unto him for righteousness.' [4] Now to him that worketh is the reward not reckoned of grace, but of debt. [5] But to him that worketh not, but believeth on him that justifieth the ungodly, his faith is counted for righteousness. [6] Even as David also describeth the blessedness of the man, unto whom God imputeth righteousness without works, [7] saying, 'Blessed are they whose iniquities are forgiven, and whose sins are covered. [8] Blessed is the man to whom the Lord will not impute sin.'

[9] Cometh this blessedness then upon the circumcision only, or upon the uncircumcision also? For we say that faith was reckoned to Abraham for righteousness. [10] How was it then reckoned? When he was in circumcision, or in uncircumcision? Not in circumcision, but in uncircumcision. [11] And he received the sign of circumcision, a seal of the righteousness of the faith which he had yet being uncircumcised, that he might be the father of all them that believe, though they be not circumcised, that righteousness might be imputed unto them also: [12] and the father of circumcision to them who are not of the circumcision only, but who also walk in the steps of that faith of our father Abraham, which he had being yet uncircumcised.

¹³ For the promise, that he should be the heir of the world, was not to Abraham, or to his seed, through the law, but through the righteousness of faith. ¹⁴ For if they which are of the law be heirs, faith is made void, and the promise made of none effect, ¹⁵ because the law worketh wrath, for where no law is, there is no transgression.

¹⁶ Therefore it is of faith, that it might be by grace; to the end the promise might be sure to all the seed; not to that only which is of the law, but to that also which is of the faith of Abraham; who is the father of us all ¹⁷(as it is written, I have made thee a father of many nations), before him whom he believed, even, God, who quickeneth the dead, and calleth those things which be not as though they were. ¹⁸ Who against hope believed in hope, that he might become the father of many nations, according to that which was spoken, 'So shall thy seed be.' ¹⁹And being not weak in faith, he considered not his own body now dead, when he was about an hundred years old, neither yet the deadness of Sara's womb: ²⁰he staggered not at the promise of God through unbelief; but was strong in faith, giving glory to God; ²¹and being fully persuaded that, what he had promised, he was able also to perform. ²²And therefore it was imputed to him for righteousness. ²³ Now it was not written for his sake alone, that it was imputed to him; ²⁴ but for us also, to whom it shall be imputed, if we believe on him that raised up Jesus our Lord from the dead; ²⁵ who was delivered for our offences, and was raised again for our justification.

5 Therefore being justified by faith, we have peace with God through our Lord Jesus Christ, ² by whom also we have access by faith into this grace wherein we stand, and rejoice in

hope of the glory of God. ³And not only so, but we glory in tribulations also: knowing that tribulation worketh patience; ⁴and patience, experience; and experience, hope: ⁵and hope maketh not ashamed, because the love of God is shed abroad in our hearts by the Holy Ghost which is given unto us.

⁶For when we were yet without strength, in due time Christ died for the ungodly. ⁷For scarcely for a righteous man will one die: yet peradventure for a good man some would even dare to die. ⁸But God commendeth his love toward us, in that, while we were yet sinners, Christ died for us. ⁹Much more then, being now justified by his blood, we shall be saved from wrath through him. ¹⁰For if, when we were enemies, we were reconciled to God by the death of his Son, much more, being reconciled, we shall be saved by his life. ¹¹And not only so, but we also joy in God through our Lord Jesus Christ, by whom we have now received the atonement.

¹²Wherefore, as by one man sin entered into the world, and death by sin; and so death passed upon all men, for that all have sinned. ¹³For until the law sin was in the world, but sin is not imputed when there is no law. ¹⁴Nevertheless death reigned from Adam to Moses, even over them that had not sinned after the similitude of Adam's transgression, who is the figure of him that was to come.

¹⁵But not as the offence, so also is the free gift. For if through the offence of one many be dead, much more the grace of God, and the gift by grace, which is by one man, Jesus Christ, hath abounded unto many. ¹⁶And not as it was by one that sinned, so is the gift, for the judgment was by one to condemnation, but the free gift is of many offences unto justification. ¹⁷For if by one man's offence death reigned by one; much more they which

receive abundance of grace and of the gift of righteousness shall reign in life by one, Jesus Christ.)

[18] Therefore as by the offence of one judgment came upon all men to condemnation; even so by the righteousness of one the free gift came upon all men unto justification of life. [19] For as by one man's disobedience many were made sinners, so by the obedience of one shall many be made righteous. [20] Moreover the law entered, that the offence might abound. But where sin abounded, grace did much more abound, [21] that as sin hath reigned unto death, even so might grace reign through righteousness unto eternal life by Jesus Christ our Lord.

6 What shall we say then? Shall we continue in sin, that grace may abound? [2] God forbid. How shall we, that are dead to sin, live any longer therein? [3] Know ye not, that so many of us as were baptized into Jesus Christ were baptized into his death? [4] Therefore we are buried with him by baptism into death, that like as Christ was raised up from the dead by the glory of the Father, even so we also should walk in newness of life.

[5] For if we have been planted together in the likeness of his death, we shall be also in the likeness of his resurrection, [6] knowing this, that our old man is crucified with him, that the body of sin might be destroyed, that henceforth we should not serve sin. [7] For he that is dead is freed from sin. [8] Now if we be dead with Christ, we believe that we shall also live with him, [9] knowing that Christ being raised from the dead dieth no more; death hath no more dominion over him. [10] For in that he died, he died unto sin once; but in that he liveth, he liveth unto God. [11] Likewise reckon ye also yourselves to be dead indeed unto sin, but alive unto God through Jesus Christ our Lord.

^{12} Let not sin therefore reign in your mortal body, that ye should obey it in the lusts thereof. ^{13} Neither yield ye your members as instruments of unrighteousness unto sin; but yield yourselves unto God, as those that are alive from the dead, and your members as instruments of righteousness unto God. ^{14} For sin shall not have dominion over you, for ye are not under the law, but under grace.

^{15} What then? Shall we sin, because we are not under the law, but under grace? God forbid. ^{16} Know ye not, that to whom ye yield yourselves servants to obey, his servants ye are to whom ye obey; whether of sin unto death, or of obedience unto righteousness? ^{17} But God be thanked, that ye were the servants of sin, but ye have obeyed from the heart that form of doctrine which was delivered you. ^{18} Being then made free from sin, ye became the servants of righteousness. ^{19} I speak after the manner of men because of the infirmity of your flesh, for as ye have yielded your members servants to uncleanness and to iniquity unto iniquity; even so now yield your members servants to righteousness unto holiness.

^{20} For when ye were the servants of sin, ye were free from righteousness. ^{21} What fruit had ye then in those things whereof ye are now ashamed? For the end of those things is death. ^{22} But now being made free from sin, and become servants to God, ye have your fruit unto holiness, and the end everlasting life. ^{23} For the wages of sin is death; but the gift of God is eternal life through Jesus Christ our Lord.

7 Know ye not, brethren (for I speak to them that know the law), how that the law hath dominion over a man as long as he liveth? ^{2} For the woman which hath an husband is bound by

the law to her husband so long as he liveth; but if the husband be dead, she is loosed from the law of her husband. ³So then if, while her husband liveth, she be married to another man, she shall be called an adulteress: but if her husband be dead, she is free from that law; so that she is no adulteress, though she be married to another man.

⁴Wherefore, my brethren, ye also are become dead to the law by the body of Christ; that ye should be married to another, even to him who is raised from the dead, that we should bring forth fruit unto God. ⁵For when we were in the flesh, the motions of sins, which were by the law, did work in our members to bring forth fruit unto death. ⁶But now we are delivered from the law, that being dead wherein we were held; that we should serve in newness of spirit, and not in the oldness of the letter.

⁷What shall we say then? Is the law sin? God forbid. Nay, I had not known sin, but by the law, for I had not known lust, except the law had said, 'Thou shalt not covet.' ⁸But sin, taking occasion by the commandment, wrought in me all manner of concupiscence. For without the law sin was dead. ⁹For I was alive without the law once: but when the commandment came, sin revived, and I died. ¹⁰And the commandment, which was ordained to life, I found to be unto death. ¹¹For sin, taking occasion by the commandment, deceived me, and by it slew me. ¹²Wherefore the law is holy, and the commandment holy, and just, and good.

¹³Was then that which is good made death unto me? God forbid. But sin, that it might appear sin, working death in me by that which is good; that sin by the commandment might become exceeding sinful.

¹⁴ For we know that the law is spiritual: but I am carnal, sold under sin. ¹⁵ For that which I do I allow not; for what I would, that do I not; but what I hate, that do I. ¹⁶ If then I do that which I would not, I consent unto the law that it is good. ¹⁷ Now then it is no more I that do it, but sin that dwelleth in me. ¹⁸ For I know that in me (that is, in my flesh), dwelleth no good thing, for to will is present with me; but how to perform that which is good I find not. ¹⁹ For the good that I would I do not, but the evil which I would not, that I do. ²⁰ Now if I do that I would not, it is no more I that do it, but sin that dwelleth in me.

²¹ I find then a law, that, when I would do good, evil is present with me. ²² For I delight in the law of God after the inward man, ²³ but I see another law in my members, warring against the law of my mind, and bringing me into captivity to the law of sin which is in my members. ²⁴ O wretched man that I am! Who shall deliver me from the body of this death? ²⁵ I thank God through Jesus Christ our Lord. So then with the mind I myself serve the law of God; but with the flesh the law of sin.

8 There is therefore now no condemnation to them which are in Christ Jesus, who walk not after the flesh, but after the Spirit. ² For the law of the Spirit of life in Christ Jesus hath made me free from the law of sin and death. ³ For what the law could not do, in that it was weak through the flesh, God sending his own Son in the likeness of sinful flesh, and for sin, condemned sin in the flesh, ⁴ that the righteousness of the law might be fulfilled in us, who walk not after the flesh, but after the Spirit. ⁵ For they that are after the flesh do mind the things of the flesh; but they that are after the Spirit the things of the Spirit. ⁶ For to be carnally minded is death; but to be spiritually minded is life and

peace. [7] Because the carnal mind is enmity against God, for it is not subject to the law of God, neither indeed can be. [8] So then they that are in the flesh cannot please God.

[9] But ye are not in the flesh, but in the Spirit, if so be that the Spirit of God dwell in you. Now if any man have not the Spirit of Christ, he is none of his. [10] And if Christ be in you, the body is dead because of sin; but the Spirit is life because of righteousness. [11] But if the Spirit of him that raised up Jesus from the dead dwell in you, he that raised up Christ from the dead shall also quicken your mortal bodies by his Spirit that dwelleth in you.

[12] Therefore, brethren, we are debtors, not to the flesh, to live after the flesh. [13] For if ye live after the flesh, ye shall die, but if ye through the Spirit do mortify the deeds of the body, ye shall live. [14] For as many as are led by the Spirit of God, they are the sons of God. [15] For ye have not received the spirit of bondage again to fear; but ye have received the Spirit of adoption, whereby we cry, 'Abba, Father.' [16] The Spirit itself beareth witness with our spirit, that we are the children of God: [17] and if children, then heirs; heirs of God, and joint-heirs with Christ; if so be that we suffer with him, that we may be also glorified together.

[18] For I reckon that the sufferings of this present time are not worthy to be compared with the glory which shall be revealed in us. [19] For the earnest expectation of the creature waiteth for the manifestation of the sons of God. [20] For the creature was made subject to vanity, not willingly, but by reason of him who hath subjected the same in hope, [21] because the creature itself also shall be delivered from the bondage of corruption into the glorious liberty of the children of God. [22] For we know that the whole creation groaneth and travaileth in pain together until now. [23] And not only they, but ourselves also, which have the

firstfruits of the Spirit, even we ourselves groan within ourselves, waiting for the adoption, to wit, the redemption of our body. ²⁴ For we are saved by hope, but hope that is seen is not hope, for what a man seeth, why doth he yet hope for? ²⁵ But if we hope for that we see not, then do we with patience wait for it.

²⁶ Likewise the Spirit also helpeth our infirmities, for we know not what we should pray for as we ought, but the Spirit itself maketh intercession for us with groanings which cannot be uttered. ²⁷ And he that searcheth the hearts knoweth what is the mind of the Spirit, because he maketh intercession for the saints according to the will of God.

²⁸ And we know that all things work together for good to them that love God, to them who are the called according to his purpose. ²⁹ For whom he did foreknow, he also did predestinate to be conformed to the image of his Son, that he might be the firstborn among many brethren. ³⁰ Moreover whom he did predestinate, them he also called: and whom he called, them he also justified: and whom he justified, them he also glorified. ³¹ What shall we then say to these things? If God be for us, who can be against us? ³² He that spared not his own Son, but delivered him up for us all, how shall he not with him also freely give us all things? ³³ Who shall lay any thing to the charge of God's elect? It is God that justifieth. ³⁴ Who is he that condemneth? It is Christ that died, yea rather, that is risen again, who is even at the right hand of God, who also maketh intercession for us. ³⁵ Who shall separate us from the love of Christ? Shall tribulation, or distress, or persecution, or famine, or nakedness, or peril, or sword? ³⁶ As it is written, 'For thy sake we are killed all the day long; we are accounted as sheep for the slaughter.'

³⁷ Nay, in all these things we are more than conquerors through him that loved us. ³⁸ For I am persuaded, that neither death, nor life, nor angels, nor principalities, nor powers, nor things present, nor things to come, ³⁹ nor height, nor depth, nor any other creature, shall be able to separate us from the love of God, which is in Christ Jesus our Lord.

9 I say the truth in Christ, I lie not, my conscience also bearing me witness in the Holy Ghost, ² that I have great heaviness and continual sorrow in my heart. ³ For I could wish that myself were accursed from Christ for my brethren, my kinsmen according to the flesh, ⁴ who are Israelites; to whom pertaineth the adoption, and the glory, and the covenants, and the giving of the law, and the service of God, and the promises; ⁵ whose are the fathers, and of whom as concerning the flesh Christ came, who is over all, God blessed for ever. Amen.

⁶ Not as though the word of God hath taken none effect. For they are not all Israel, which are of Israel: ⁷ neither, because they are the seed of Abraham, are they all children, but, 'In Isaac shall thy seed be called.' ⁸ That is, 'They which are the children of the flesh, these are not the children of God, but the children of the promise are counted for the seed.' ⁹ For this is the word of promise, 'At this time will I come, and Sara shall have a son.' ¹⁰ And not only this; but when Rebecca also had conceived by one, even by our father Isaac. ¹¹ (For the children being not yet born, neither having done any good or evil, that the purpose of God according to election might stand, not of works, but of him that calleth.) ¹² It was said unto her, 'The elder shall serve the younger.' ¹³ As it is written, 'Jacob have I loved, but Esau have I hated.'

¹⁴ What shall we say then? Is there unrighteousness with God? God forbid. ¹⁵ For he saith to Moses, 'I will have mercy on whom I will have mercy, and I will have compassion on whom I will have compassion.' ¹⁶ So then it is not of him that willeth, nor of him that runneth, but of God that sheweth mercy. ¹⁷ For the scripture saith unto Pharaoh, 'Even for this same purpose have I raised thee up, that I might shew my power in thee, and that my name might be declared throughout all the earth.' ¹⁸ Therefore hath he mercy on whom he will have mercy, and whom he will he hardeneth.

¹⁹ Thou wilt say then unto me, 'Why doth he yet find fault? For who hath resisted his will?' ²⁰ Nay but, O man, who art thou that repliest against God? Shall the thing formed say to him that formed it, 'Why hast thou made me thus?' ²¹ Hath not the potter power over the clay, of the same lump to make one vessel unto honour, and another unto dishonour? ²² What if God, willing to shew his wrath, and to make his power known, endured with much longsuffering the vessels of wrath fitted to destruction; ²³ and that he might make known the riches of his glory on the vessels of mercy, which he had afore prepared unto glory, ²⁴ even us, whom he hath called, not of the Jews only, but also of the Gentiles? ²⁵ As he saith also in Osee, 'I will call them "my people", which were not my people; and her "beloved", which was not beloved.' ²⁶ And it shall come to pass, that in the place where it was said unto them, "Ye are not my people"; there shall they be called the children of the living God.'

²⁷ Esaias also crieth concerning Israel, 'Though the number of the children of Israel be as the sand of the sea, a remnant shall be saved, ²⁸ for he will finish the work, and cut it short in righteousness, because a short work will the Lord make upon the earth.'

²⁹ And as Esaias said before, 'Except the Lord of Sabaoth had left us a seed, we had been as Sodoma, and been made like unto Gomorrha.'

³⁰ What shall we say then? That the Gentiles, which followed not after righteousness, have attained to righteousness, even the righteousness which is of faith. ³¹ But Israel, which followed after the law of righteousness, hath not attained to the law of righteousness. ³² Wherefore? Because they sought it not by faith, but as it were by the works of the law. For they stumbled at that stumblingstone; ³³ as it is written, 'Behold, I lay in Sion a stumblingstone and rock of offence: and whosoever believeth on him shall not be ashamed.'

10 Brethren, my heart's desire and prayer to God for Israel is, that they might be saved. ² For I bear them record that they have a zeal of God, but not according to knowledge. ³ For they being ignorant of God's righteousness, and going about to establish their own righteousness, have not submitted themselves unto the righteousness of God. ⁴ For Christ is the end of the law for righteousness to every one that believeth.

⁵ For Moses describeth the righteousness which is of the law, 'That the man which doeth those things shall live by them.' ⁶ But the righteousness which is of faith speaketh on this wise, 'Say not in thine heart, "Who shall ascend into heaven?" (that is, to bring Christ down from above) ⁷ Or, "Who shall descend into the deep?"' (That is, to bring up Christ again from the dead.) ⁸ But what saith it? The word is nigh thee, even in thy mouth, and in thy heart: that is, the word of faith, which we preach; ⁹ that if thou shalt confess with thy mouth the Lord Jesus, and shalt believe in thine heart that God hath raised him from the

dead, thou shalt be saved. ^{10} For with the heart man believeth unto righteousness; and with the mouth confession is made unto salvation. ^{11} For the scripture saith, 'Whosoever believeth on him shall not be ashamed.' ^{12} For there is no difference between the Jew and the Greek, for the same Lord over all is rich unto all that call upon him. ^{13} For whosoever shall call upon the name of the Lord shall be saved.

^{14} How then shall they call on him in whom they have not believed? And how shall they believe in him of whom they have not heard? And how shall they hear without a preacher? ^{15} And how shall they preach, except they be sent? As it is written, 'How beautiful are the feet of them that preach the gospel of peace, and bring glad tidings of good things!' ^{16} But they have not all obeyed the gospel. For Esaias saith, 'Lord, who hath believed our report?' ^{17} So then faith cometh by hearing, and hearing by the word of God.

^{18} But I say, 'Have they not heard? Yes verily, their sound went into all the earth, and their words unto the ends of the world.' ^{19} But I say, 'Did not Israel know?' First Moses saith, 'I will provoke you to jealousy by them that are no people, and by a foolish nation I will anger you.' ^{20} But Esaias is very bold, and saith, 'I was found of them that sought me not; I was made manifest unto them that asked not after me.' ^{21} But to Israel he saith, 'All day long I have stretched forth my hands unto a disobedient and gainsaying people.'

11 I say then, 'Hath God cast away his people?' God forbid. For I also am an Israelite, of the seed of Abraham, of the tribe of Benjamin. ^{2} God hath not cast away his people which he foreknew. Wot ye not what the scripture saith of Elias? How he maketh intercession to God against Israel, saying, ³'Lord, they have killed thy prophets, and digged down thine altars; and I am left alone, and they seek my life.' ⁴But what saith the answer of God unto him? 'I have reserved to myself seven thousand men, who have not bowed the knee to the image of Baal.' ⁵Even so then at this present time also there is a remnant according to the election of grace. ⁶And if by grace, then is it no more of works: otherwise grace is no more grace. But if it be of works, then is it no more grace: otherwise work is no more work.

⁷What then? Israel hath not obtained that which he seeketh for; but the election hath obtained it, and the rest were blinded ⁸according as it is written, 'God hath given them the spirit of slumber, eyes that they should not see, and ears that they should not hear unto this day. ⁹And David saith, Let their table be made a snare, and a trap, and a stumbling-block, and a recompence unto them: ¹⁰let their eyes be darkened, that they may not see, and bow down their back alway.'

¹¹I say then, 'Have they stumbled that they should fall?' God forbid: but rather through their fall salvation is come unto the Gentiles, for to provoke them to jealousy. ¹²Now if the fall of them be the riches of the world, and the diminishing of them the riches of the Gentiles; how much more their fulness?

¹³For I speak to you Gentiles, inas-much as I am the apostle of the Gentiles, I magnify mine office: ¹⁴if by any means I may provoke to emulation them which are my flesh, and might save some of them. ¹⁵For if the casting away of them be the reconciling of the world, what shall the receiving of them be, but life from the dead? ¹⁶For if the firstfruit be holy, the lump is also holy: and if the root be holy, so are the branches.

¹⁷And if some of the branches be broken off, and thou, being a wild olive tree, wert graffed in among them, and with them partakest of the root and fatness of the olive tree; ¹⁸boast not against the branches. But if thou boast, thou bearest not the root, but the root thee. ¹⁹Thou wilt say then, 'The branches were broken off, that I might be graffed in.' ²⁰Well; because of unbelief they were broken off, and thou standest by faith. 'Be not highminded, but fear, ²¹for if God spared not the natural branches, take heed lest he also spare not thee. ²²Behold therefore the goodness and severity of God: on them which fell, severity; but toward thee, goodness, if thou continue in his goodness: otherwise thou also shalt be cut off. ²³And they also, if they abide not still in unbelief, shall be graffed in, for God is able to graff them in again. ²⁴For if thou wert cut out of the olive tree which is wild by nature, and wert graffed contrary to nature into a good olive tree, how much more shall these, which be the natural branches, be graffed into their own olive tree?

²⁵For I would not, brethren, that ye should be ignorant of this mystery, lest ye should be wise in your own conceits; that blindness in part is happened to Israel, until the fulness of the Gentiles be come in. ²⁶And so all Israel shall be saved: as it is written, 'There shall come out of Sion the Deliverer, and shall turn away ungodliness from Jacob.' ²⁷For this is my covenant unto them, when I shall take away their sins.' ²⁸As concerning the gospel, they are enemies for your sakes; but as touching the election, they are beloved for the fathers' sakes. ²⁹For the gifts and calling of God are without repentance. ³⁰For as ye in times past have not believed God, yet have now obtained mercy through their unbelief, ³¹even so have these also now not believed, that through your mercy they also may obtain mercy.

[32] For God hath concluded them all in unbelief, that he might have mercy upon all.

[33] O the depth of the riches both of the wisdom and knowledge of God! How unsearchable are his judgments, and his ways past finding out! [34] For who hath known the mind of the Lord? Or who hath been his counsellor? [35] Or who hath first given to him, and it shall be recompensed unto him again? [36] For of him, and through him, and to him, are all things: to whom be glory for ever. Amen.

12 I beseech you therefore, brethren, by the mercies of God, that ye present your bodies a living sacrifice, holy, acceptable unto God, which is your reasonable service. [2] And be not conformed to this world, but be ye transformed by the renewing of your mind, that ye may prove what is that good, and acceptable, and perfect, will of God.

[3] For I say, through the grace given unto me, to every man that is among you, not to think of himself more highly than he ought to think; but to think soberly, according as God hath dealt to every man the measure of faith. [4] For as we have many members in one body, and all members have not the same office: [5] so we, being many, are one body in Christ, and every one members one of another. [6] Having then gifts differing according to the grace that is given to us, whether prophecy, let us prophesy according to the proportion of faith; [7] or ministry, let us wait on our ministering: or he that teacheth, on teaching; [8] or he that exhorteth, on exhortation: he that giveth, let him do it with simplicity; he that ruleth, with diligence; he that sheweth mercy, with cheerfulness.

[9] Let love be without dissimulation. Abhor that which is evil;

cleave to that which is good. ¹⁰ Be kindly affectioned one to another with brotherly love; in honour preferring one another; ¹¹ not slothful in business; fervent in spirit; serving the Lord; ¹² rejoicing in hope; patient in tribulation; continuing instant in prayer; ¹³ Distributing to the necessity of saints; given to hospitality.

¹⁴ Bless them which persecute you: bless, and curse not. ¹⁵ Rejoice with them that do rejoice, and weep with them that weep. ¹⁶ Be of the same mind one toward another. Mind not high things, but condescend to men of low estate. Be not wise in your own conceits. ¹⁷ Recompense to no man evil for evil. Provide things honest in the sight of all men. ¹⁸ If it be possible, as much as lieth in you, live peaceably with all men. ¹⁹ Dearly beloved, avenge not yourselves, but rather give place unto wrath: for it is written, 'Vengeance is mine; I will repay,' saith the Lord. ²⁰ Therefore if thine enemy hunger, feed him; if he thirst, give him drink: for in so doing thou shalt heap coals of fire on his head. ²¹ Be not overcome of evil, but overcome evil with good.

13 Let every soul be subject unto the higher powers. For there is no power but of God: the powers that be are ordained of God. ² Whosoever therefore resisteth the power, resisteth the ordinance of God: and they that resist shall receive to themselves damnation. ³ For rulers are not a terror to good works, but to the evil. Wilt thou then not be afraid of the power? Do that which is good, and thou shalt have praise of the same, ⁴ for he is the minister of God to thee for good. But if thou do that which is evil, be afraid; for he beareth not the sword in vain; for he is the minister of God, a revenger to execute wrath upon him that doeth evil. ⁵ Wherefore ye must needs be subject, not only for

wrath, but also for conscience sake. ⁶For for this cause pay ye tribute also: for they are God's ministers, attending continually upon this very thing. ⁷Render therefore to all their dues: tribute to whom tribute is due; custom to whom custom; fear to whom fear; honour to whom honour.

⁸Owe no man any thing, but to love one another, for he that loveth another hath fulfilled the law. ⁹For this, 'Thou shalt not commit adultery, Thou shalt not kill, Thou shalt not steal, Thou shalt not bear false witness, Thou shalt not covet'; and if there be any other commandment, it is briefly comprehended in this saying, namely, 'Thou shalt love thy neighbour as thyself.' ¹⁰Love worketh no ill to his neighbour: therefore love is the fulfilling of the law.

¹¹And that, knowing the time, that now it is high time to awake out of sleep: for now is our salvation nearer than when we believed. ¹²The night is far spent, the day is at hand: let us therefore cast off the works of darkness, and let us put on the armour of light. ¹³Let us walk honestly, as in the day; not in rioting and drunkenness, not in chambering and wantonness, not in strife and envying. ¹⁴But put ye on the Lord Jesus Christ, and make not provision for the flesh, to fulfil the lusts thereof.

14 Him that is weak in the faith receive ye, but not to doubtful disputations. ²For one believeth that he may eat all things: another, who is weak, eateth herbs. ³Let not him that eateth despise him that eateth not; and let not him which eateth not judge him that eateth, for God hath received him. ⁴Who art thou that judgest another man's servant? To his own master he standeth or falleth. Yea, he shall be holden up, for God is able to make him stand.

⁵ One man esteemeth one day above another: another esteemeth every day alike. Let every man be fully persuaded in his own mind. ⁶ He that regardeth the day, regardeth it unto the Lord; and he that regardeth not the day, to the Lord he doth not regard it. He that eateth, eateth to the Lord, for he giveth God thanks; and he that eateth not, to the Lord he eateth not, and giveth God thanks.

⁷ For none of us liveth to himself, and no man dieth to himself. ⁸ For whether we live, we live unto the Lord; and whether we die, we die unto the Lord: whether we live therefore, or die, we are the Lord's. ⁹ For to this end Christ both died, and rose, and revived, that he might be Lord both of the dead and living.

¹⁰ But why dost thou judge thy brother? Or why dost thou set at nought thy brother? For we shall all stand before the judgment seat of Christ. ¹¹ For it is written, 'As I live,' saith the Lord, 'every knee shall bow to me, and every tongue shall confess to God.' ¹² So then every one of us shall give account of himself to God.

¹³ Let us not therefore judge one another any more, but judge this rather, that no man put a stumblingblock or an occasion to fall in his brother's way. ¹⁴ I know, and am persuaded by the Lord Jesus, that there is nothing unclean of itself, but to him that esteemeth any thing to be unclean, to him it is unclean. ¹⁵ But if thy brother be grieved with thy meat, now walkest thou not charitably. Destroy not him with thy meat, for whom Christ died. ¹⁶ Let not then your good be evil spoken of, ¹⁷ for the kingdom of God is not meat and drink; but righteousness, and peace, and joy in the Holy Ghost. ¹⁸ For he that in these things serveth Christ is acceptable to God, and approved of men. ¹⁹ Let us therefore follow after the things which make for peace, and

things wherewith one may edify another. [20] For meat destroy not the work of God. All things indeed are pure; but it is evil for that man who eateth with offence. [21] It is good neither to eat flesh, nor to drink wine, nor any thing whereby thy brother stumbleth, or is offended, or is made weak. [22] Hast thou faith? Have it to thyself before God. Happy is he that condemneth not himself in that thing which he alloweth. [23] And he that doubteth is damned if he eat, because he eateth not of faith, for whatsoever is not of faith is sin.

15

We then that are strong ought to bear the infirmities of the weak, and not to please ourselves. [2] Let every one of us please his neighbour for his good to edification. [3] For even Christ pleased not himself; but, as it is written, 'The reproaches of them that reproached thee fell on me.' [4] For whatsoever things were written aforetime were written for our learning, that we through patience and comfort of the scriptures might have hope. [5] Now the God of patience and consolation grant you to be likeminded one toward another according to Christ Jesus, [6] that ye may with one mind and one mouth glorify God, even the Father of our Lord Jesus Christ.

[7] Wherefore receive ye one another, as Christ also received us to the glory of God. [8] Now I say that Jesus Christ was a minister of the circumcision for the truth of God, to confirm the promises made unto the fathers, [9] and that the Gentiles might glorify God for his mercy; as it is written, 'For this cause I will confess to thee among the Gentiles, and sing unto thy name.' [10] And again he saith, 'Rejoice, ye Gentiles, with his people.' [11] And again, 'Praise the Lord, all ye Gentiles; and laud him, all ye people.' [12] And again, Esaias saith, 'There shall be a root of Jesse, and

he that shall rise to reign over the Gentiles; in him shall the Gentiles trust.' [13] Now the God of hope fill you with all joy and peace in believing, that ye may abound in hope, through the power of the Holy Ghost.

[14] And I myself also am persuaded of you, my brethren, that ye also are full of goodness, filled with all knowledge, able also to admonish one another. [15] Nevertheless, brethren, I have written the more boldly unto you in some sort, as putting you in mind, because of the grace that is given to me of God, [16] that I should be the minister of Jesus Christ to the Gentiles, ministering the gospel of God, that the offering up of the Gentiles might be acceptable, being sanctified by the Holy Ghost. [17] I have therefore whereof I may glory through Jesus Christ in those things which pertain to God. [18] For I will not dare to speak of any of those things which Christ hath not wrought by me, to make the Gentiles obedient, by word and deed, [19] through mighty signs and wonders, by the power of the Spirit of God; so that from Jerusalem, and round about unto Illyricum, I have fully preached the gospel of Christ. [20] Yea, so have I strived to preach the gospel, not where Christ was named, lest I should build upon another man's foundation, [21] but as it is written, 'To whom he was not spoken of, they shall see: and they that have not heard shall understand.'

[22] For which cause also I have been much hindered from coming to you. [23] But now having no more place in these parts, and having a great desire these many years to come unto you; [24] whensoever I take my journey into Spain, I will come to you, for I trust to see you in my journey, and to be brought on my way thitherward by you, if first I be somewhat filled with your company. [25] But now I go unto Jerusalem to minister unto the

saints. ²⁶ For it hath pleased them of Macedonia and Achaia to make a certain contribution for the poor saints which are at Jerusalem. ²⁷ It hath pleased them verily; and their debtors they are. For if the Gentiles have been made partakers of their spiritual things, their duty is also to minister unto them in carnal things. ²⁸ When therefore I have performed this, and have sealed to them this fruit, I will come by you into Spain. ²⁹ And I am sure that, when I come unto you, I shall come in the fulness of the blessing of the gospel of Christ.

³⁰ Now I beseech you, brethren, for the Lord Jesus Christ's sake, and for the love of the Spirit, that ye strive together with me in your prayers to God for me, ³¹ that I may be delivered from them that do not believe in Judæa; and that my service which I have for Jerusalem may be accepted of the saints; ³² that I may come unto you with joy by the will of God, and may with you be refreshed. ³³ Now the God of peace be with you all. Amen.

16 I commend unto you Phebe our sister, which is a servant of the church which is at Cenchrea: ² that ye receive her in the Lord, as becometh saints, and that ye assist her in whatsoever business she hath need of you, for she hath been a succourer of many, and of myself also.

³ Greet Priscilla and Aquila my helpers in Christ Jesus, ⁴ who have for my life laid down their own necks, unto whom not only I give thanks, but also all the churches of the Gentiles. ⁵ Likewise greet the church that is in their house. Salute my well-beloved Epænetus, who is the firstfruits of Achaia unto Christ. ⁶ Greet Mary, who bestowed much labour on us. ⁷ Salute Andronicus and Junia, my kinsmen, and my fellowprisoners,

who are of note among the apostles, who also were in Christ before me. [8]Greet Amplias my beloved in the Lord. [9]Salute Urbane, our helper in Christ, and Stachys my beloved. [10]Salute Apelles approved in Christ. Salute them which are of Aristobulus' household. [11]Salute Herodion my kinsman. Greet them that be of the household of Narcissus, which are in the Lord. [12]Salute Tryphena and Tryphosa, who labour in the Lord. Salute the beloved Persis, which laboured much in the Lord. [13]Salute Rufus chosen in the Lord, and his mother and mine. [14]Salute Asyncritus, Phlegon, Hermas, Patrobas, Hermes, and the brethren which are with them. [15]Salute Philologus, and Julia, Nereus, and his sister, and Olympas, and all the saints which are with them. [16]Salute one another with an holy kiss. The churches of Christ salute you.

[17]Now I beseech you, brethren, mark them which cause divisions and offences contrary to the doctrine which ye have learned; and avoid them. [18]For they that are such serve not our Lord Jesus Christ, but their own belly; and by good words and fair speeches deceive the hearts of the simple. [19]For your obedience is come abroad unto all men. I am glad therefore on your behalf, but yet I would have you wise unto that which is good, and simple concerning evil. [20]And the God of peace shall bruise Satan under your feet shortly. The grace of our Lord Jesus Christ be with you. Amen.

[21]Timotheus my workfellow, and Lucius, and Jason, and Sosipater, my kinsmen, salute you. [22]I Tertius, who wrote this epistle, salute you in the Lord. [23]Gaius mine host, and of the whole church, saluteth you. Erastus the chamberlain of the city saluteth you, and Quartus a brother. [24]The grace of our Lord Jesus Christ be with you all. Amen.

²⁵ Now to him that is of power to stablish you according to my gospel, and the preaching of Jesus Christ, according to the revelation of the mystery, which was kept secret since the world began, ²⁶ but now is made manifest, and by the scriptures of the prophets, according to the commandment of the everlasting God, made known to all nations for the obedience of faith: ²⁷ to God only wise, be glory through Jesus Christ for ever. Amen.